TO

FROM

DATE

Our Creator would not have made such lovely days,
and given us the deep hearts to enjoy them...
unless we were meant to be immortal.

NATHANIEL HAWTHORNE

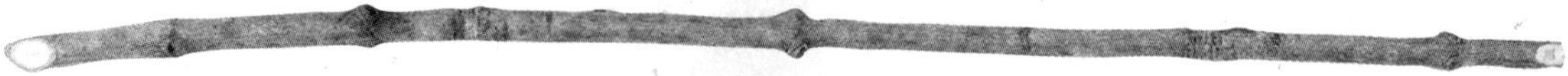

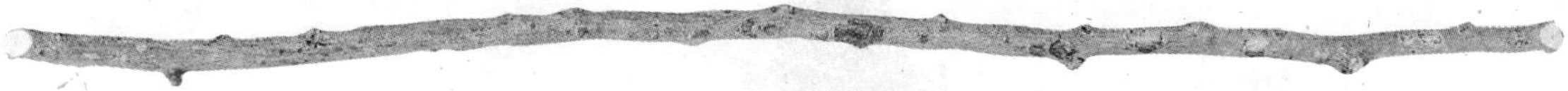

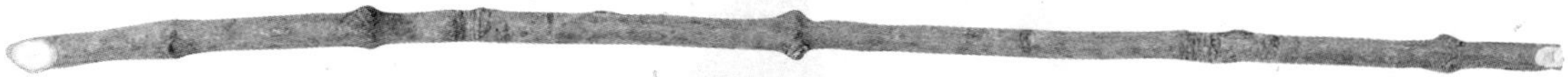

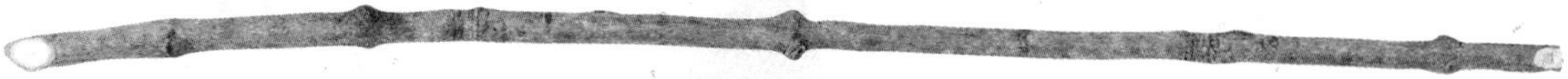

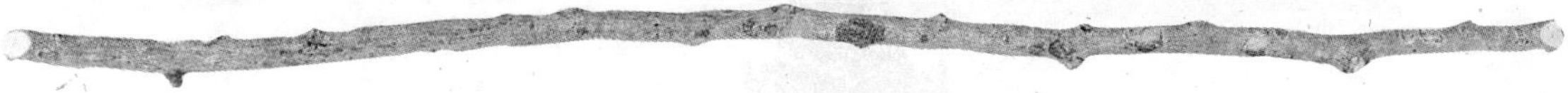

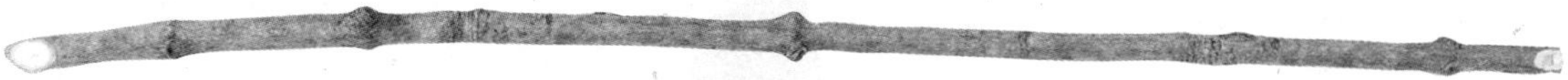

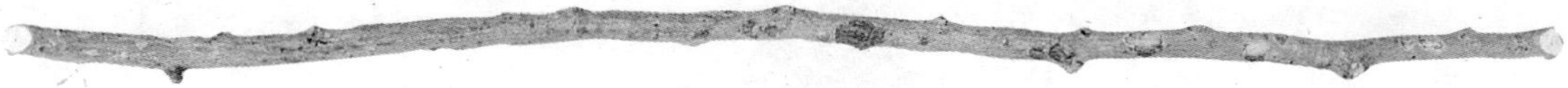

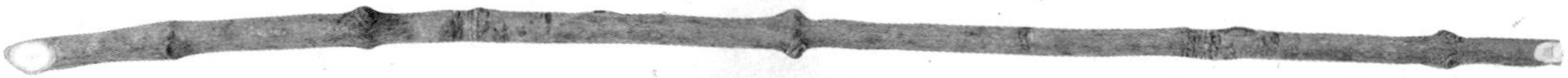

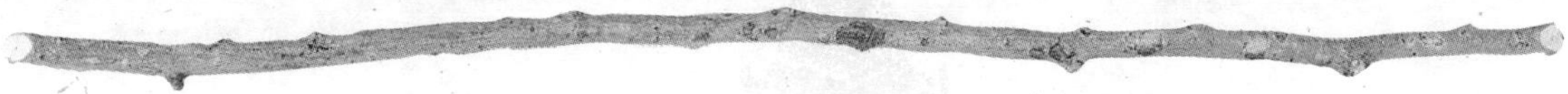

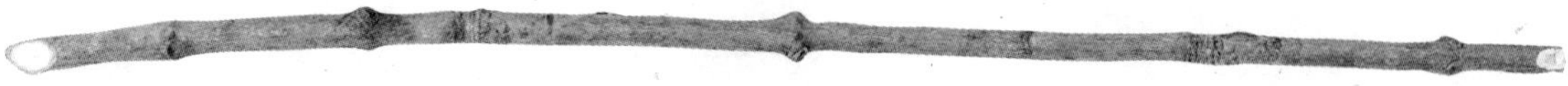

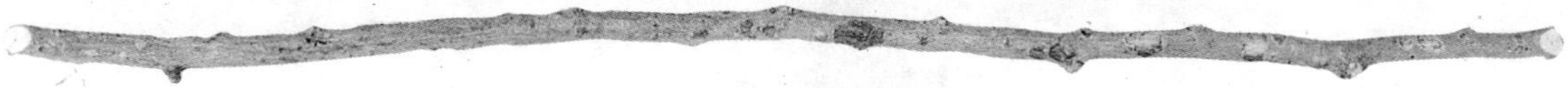

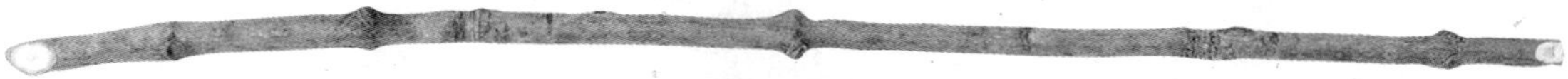

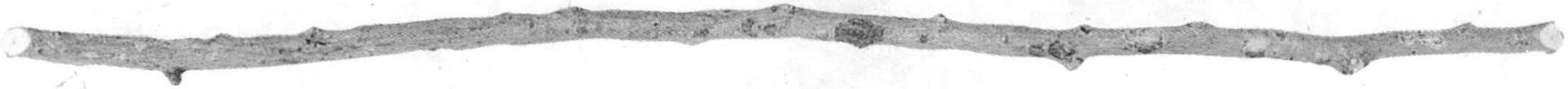

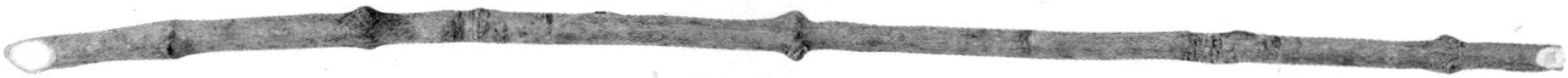

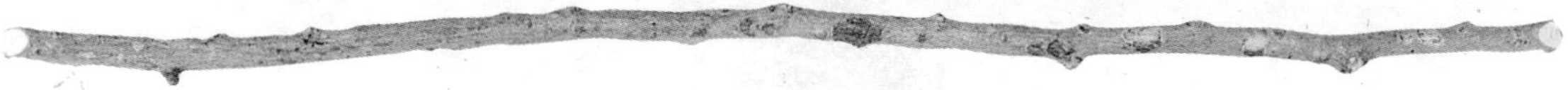

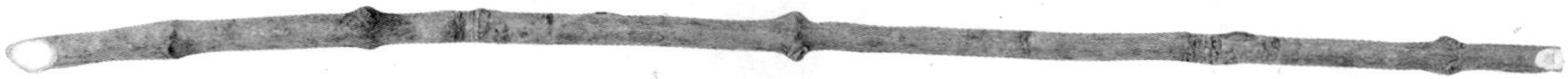

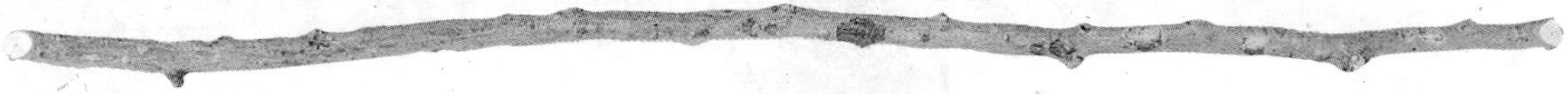

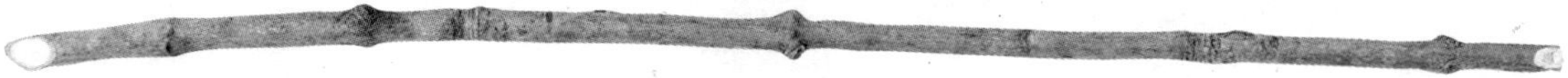

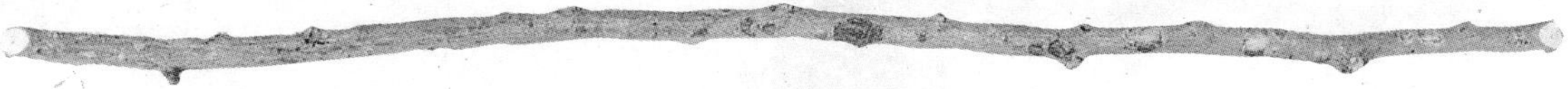

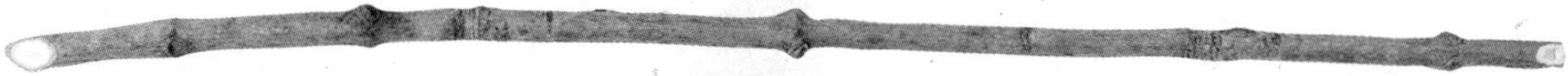

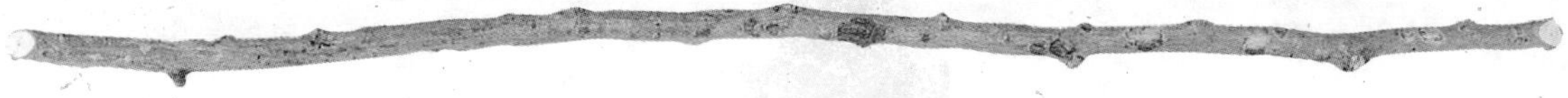

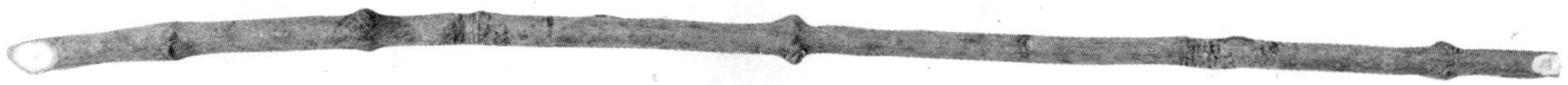

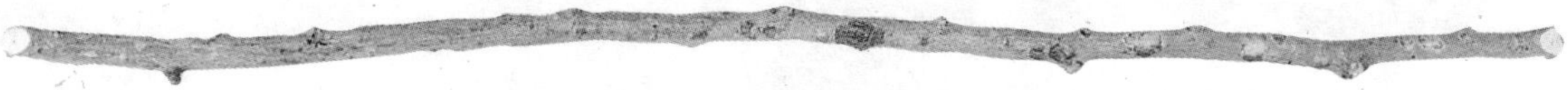

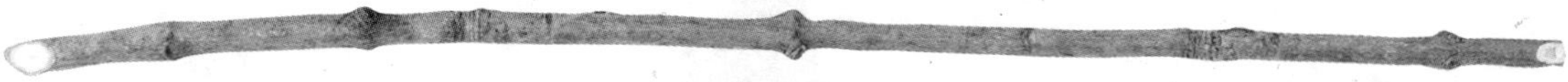

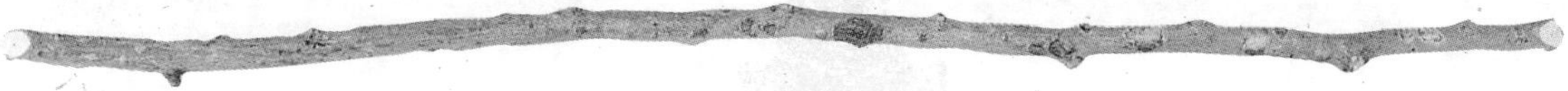

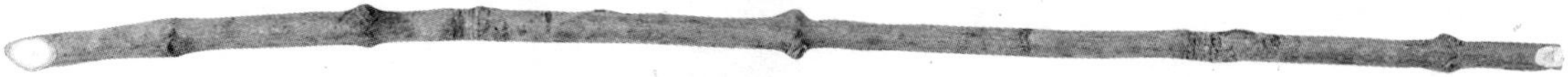

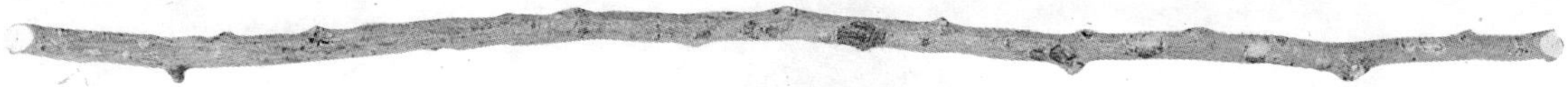

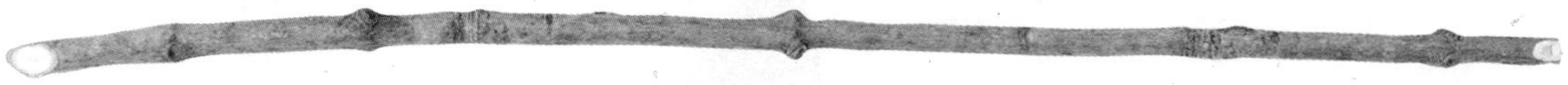

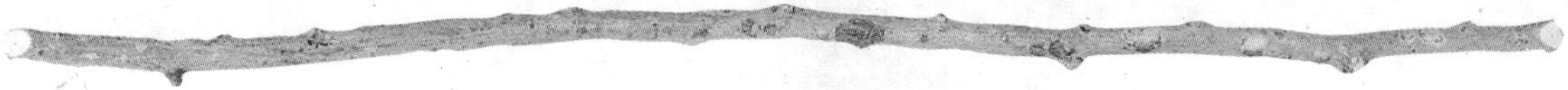

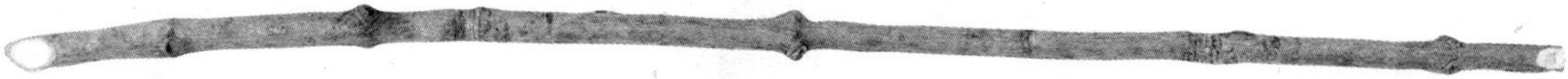

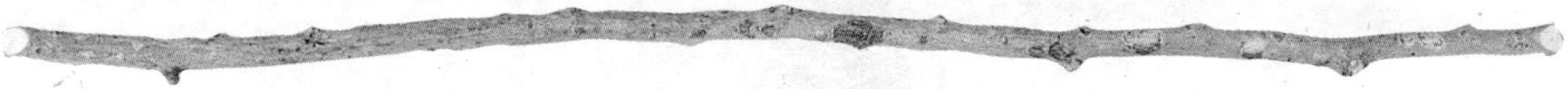

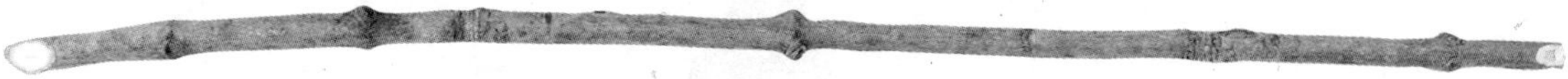

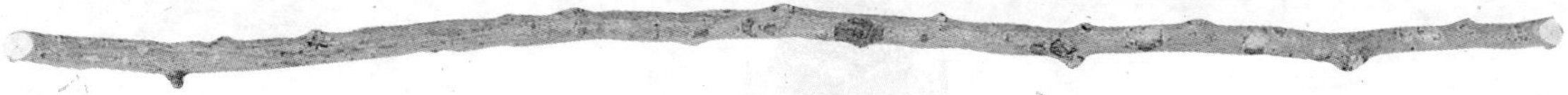

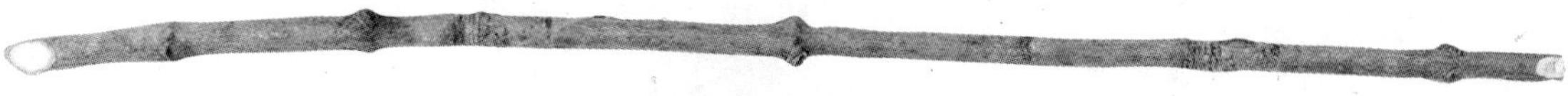

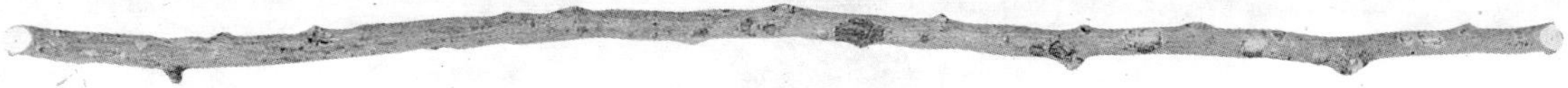

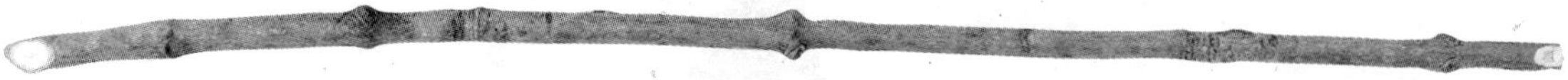

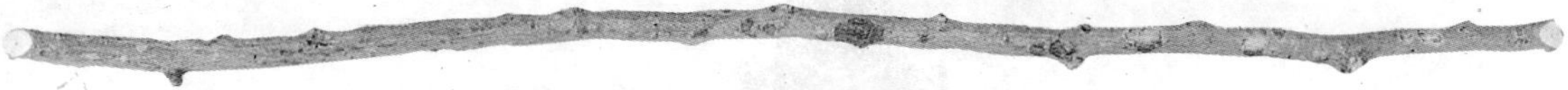

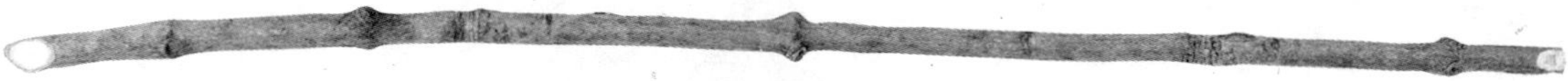

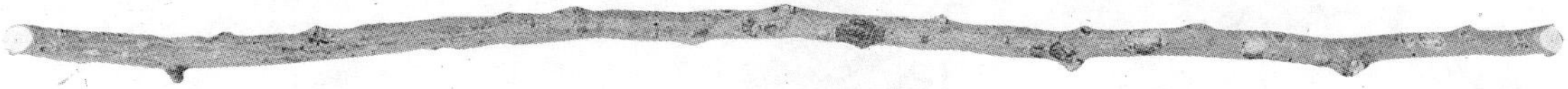

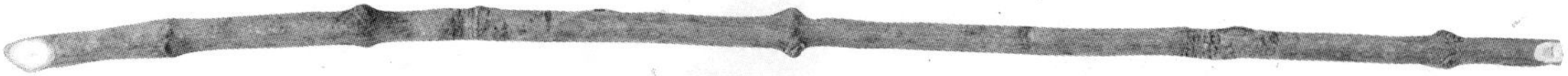

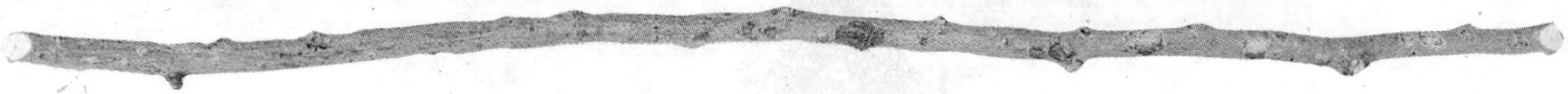

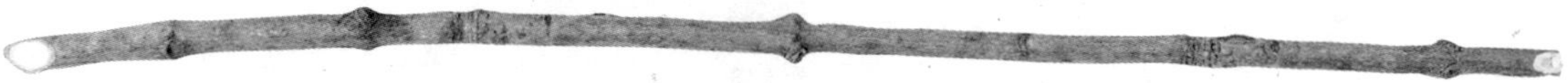

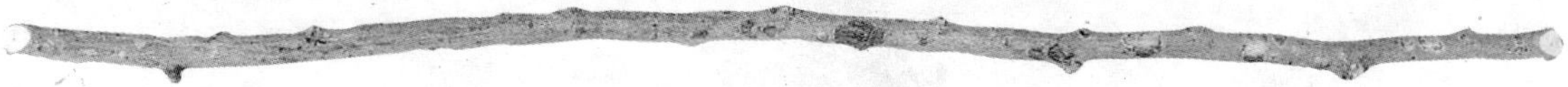

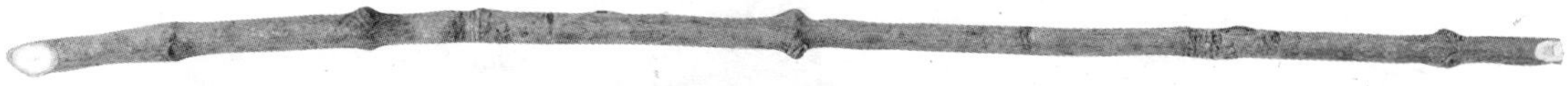

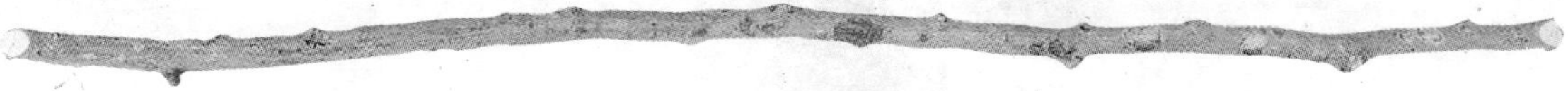

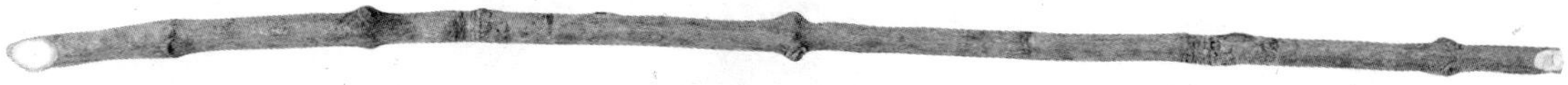

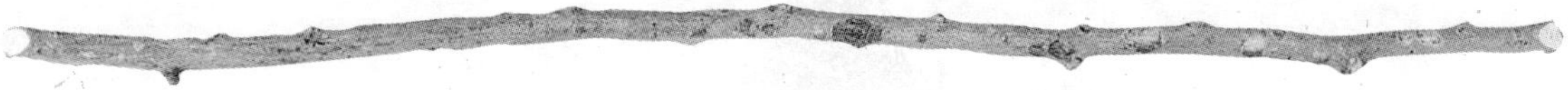

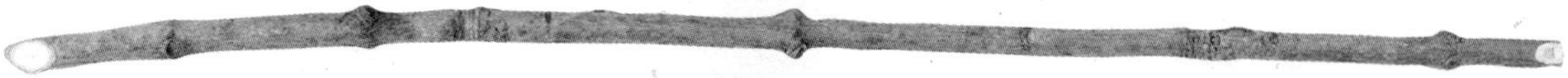

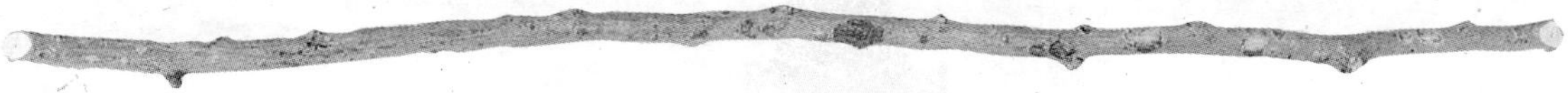

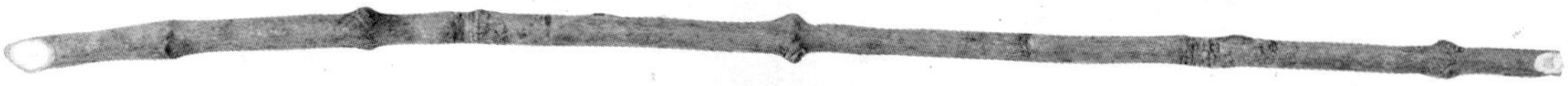

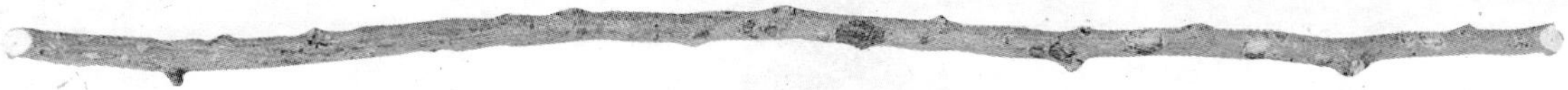

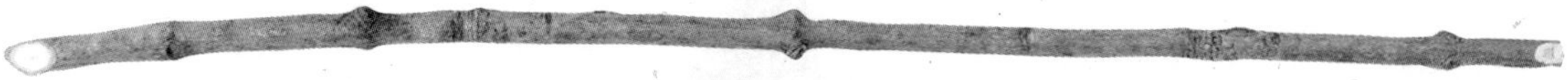

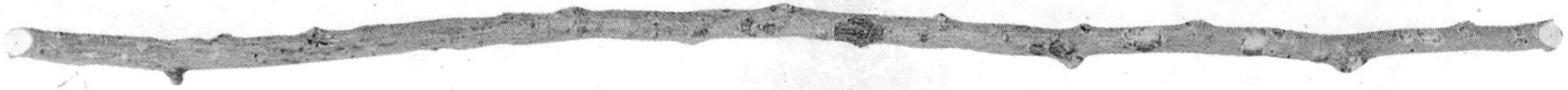

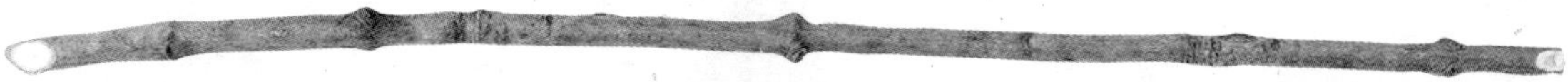

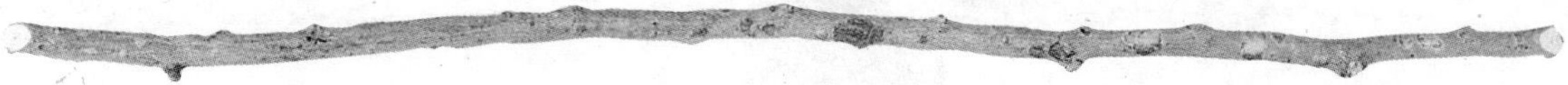

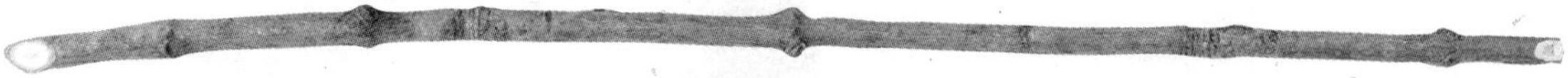

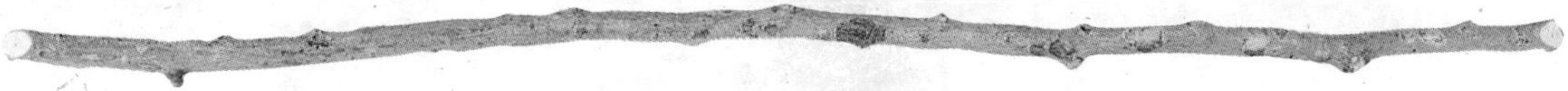

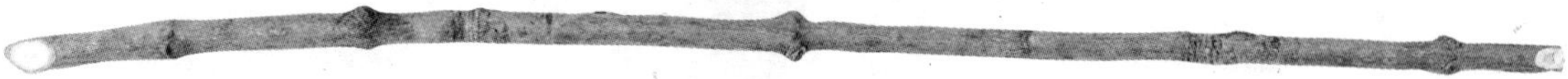

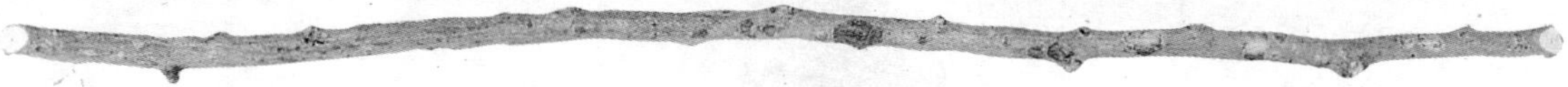

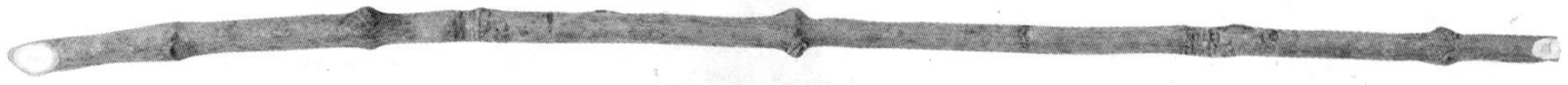

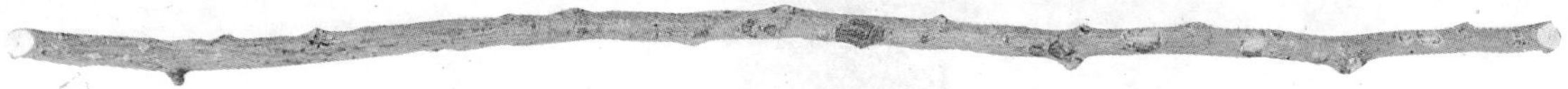

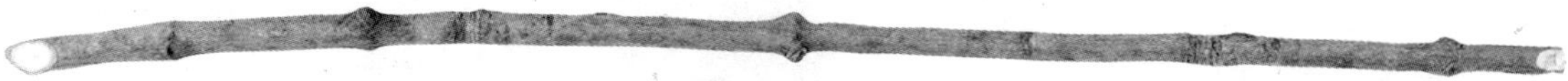

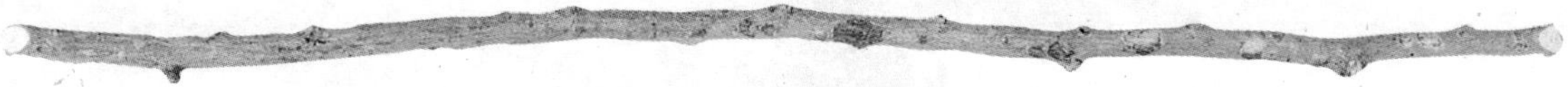

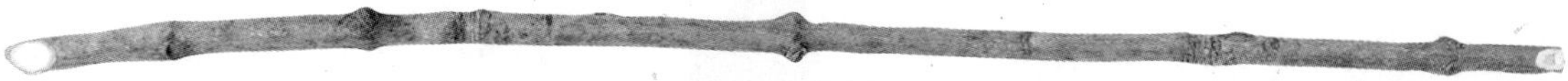

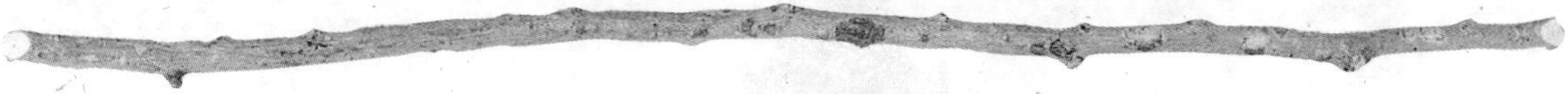

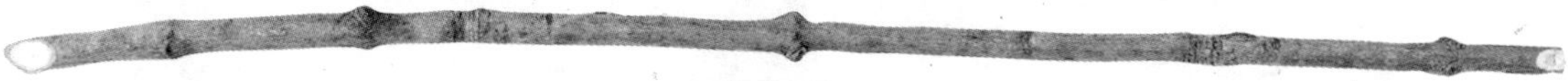

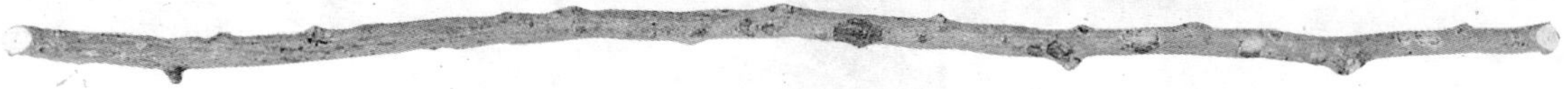

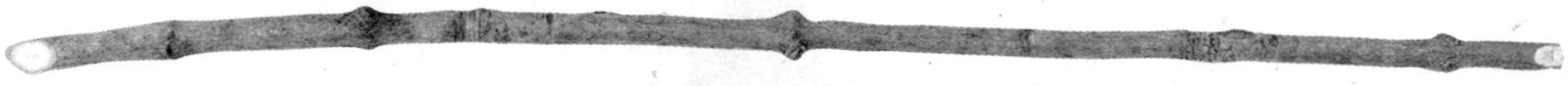

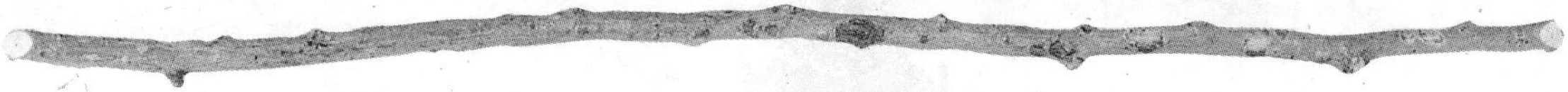

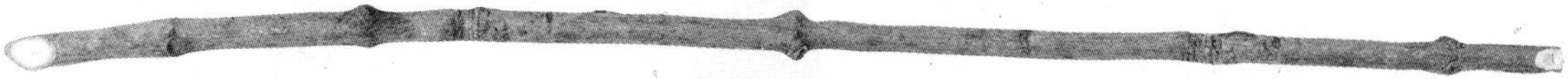

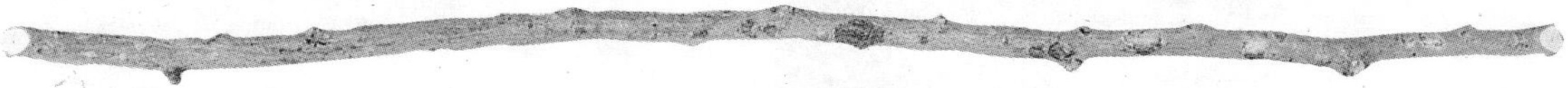

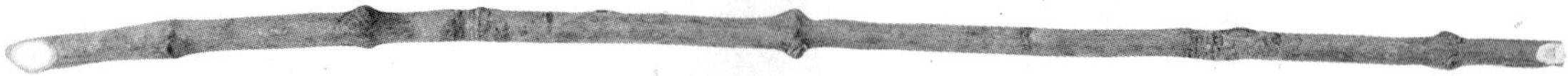

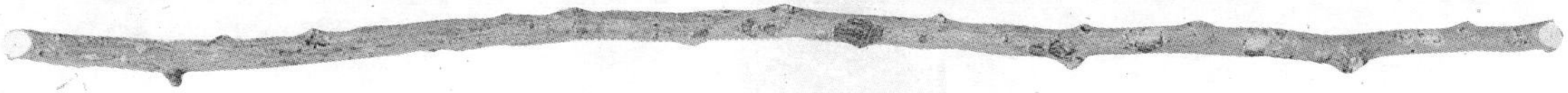

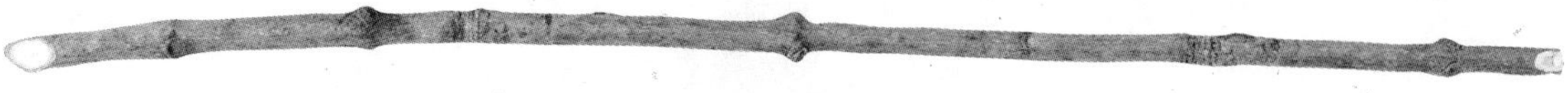

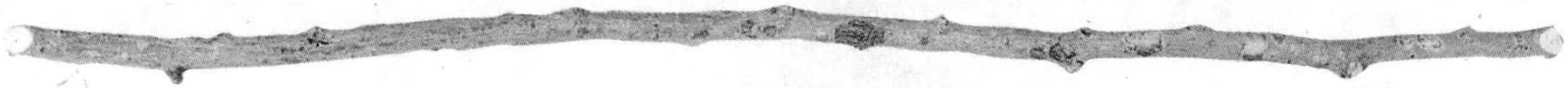

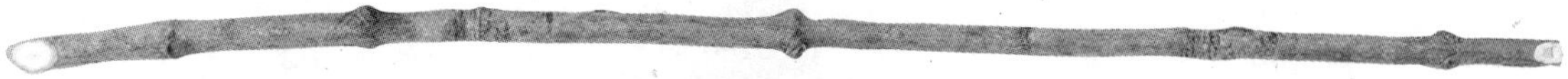

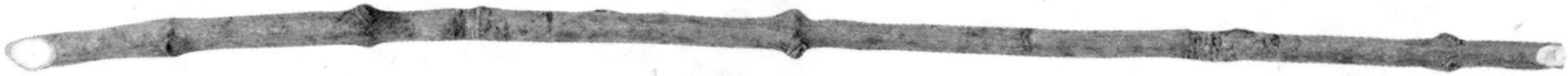

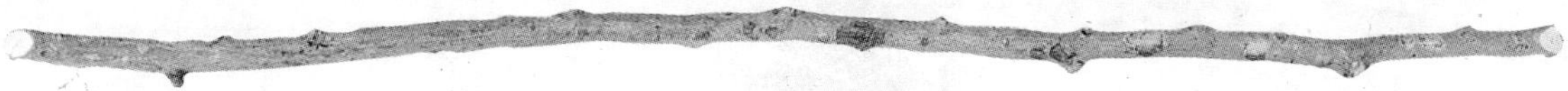

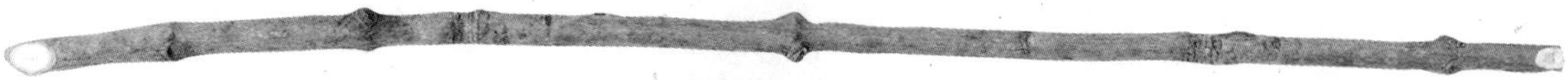

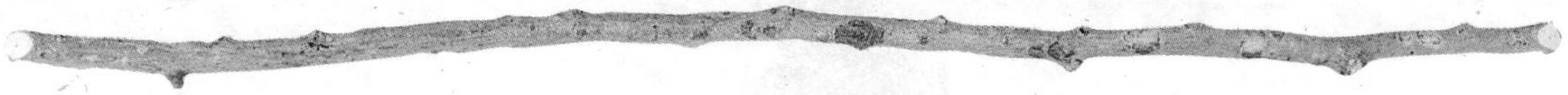

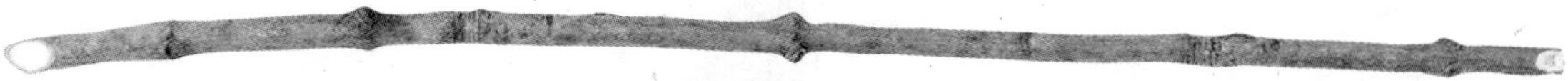

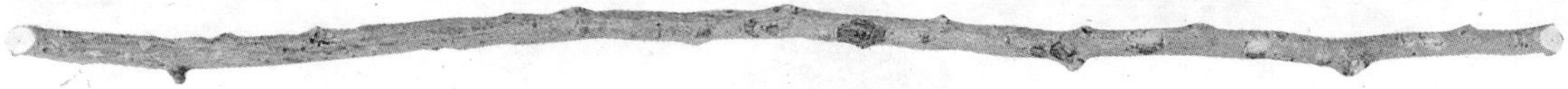

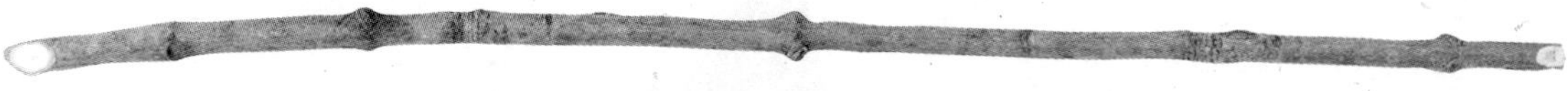

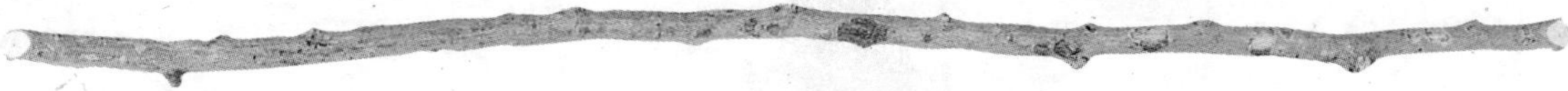

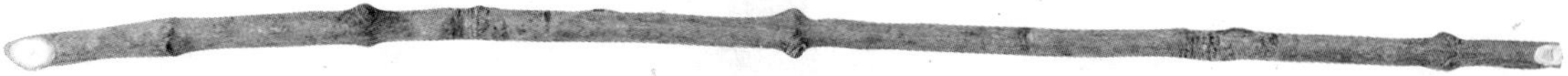

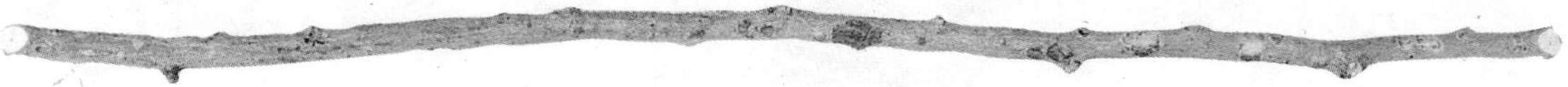

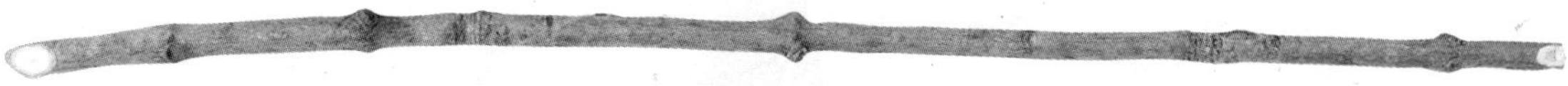

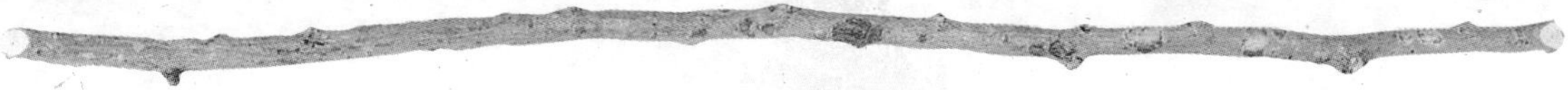

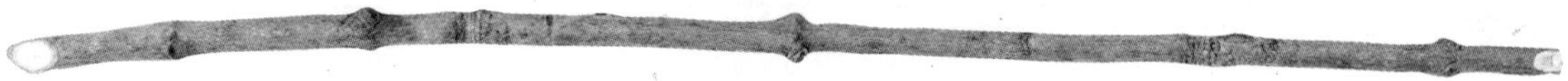

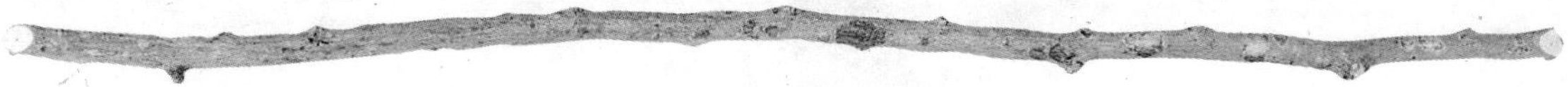

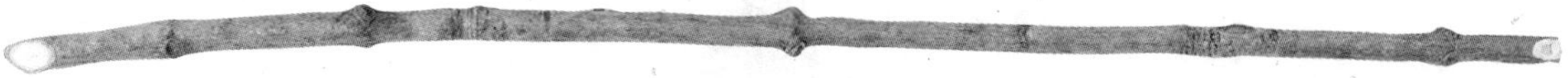

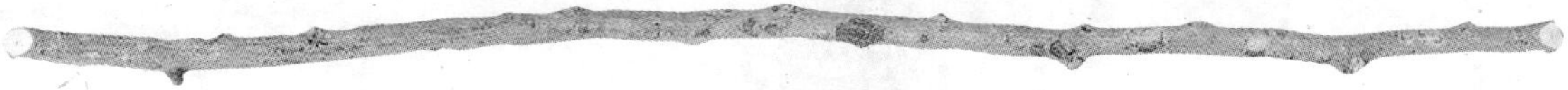

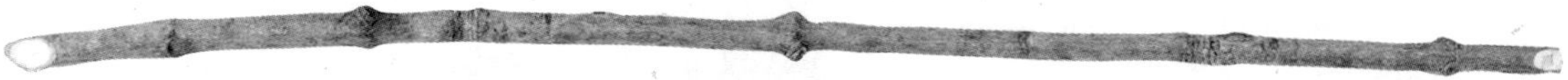

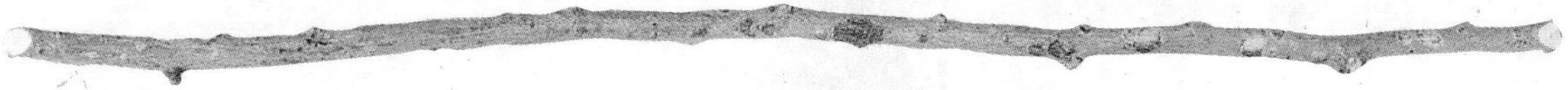

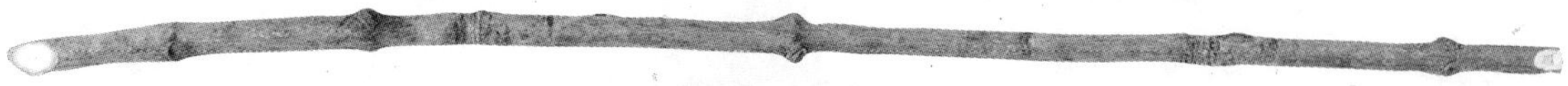

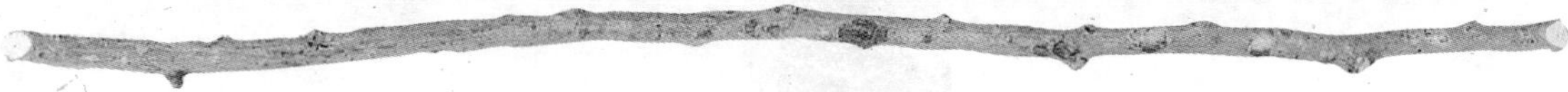

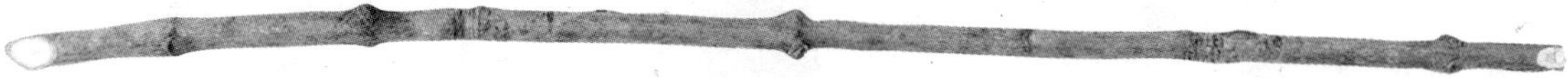

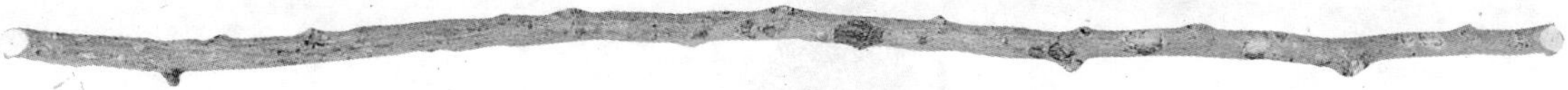

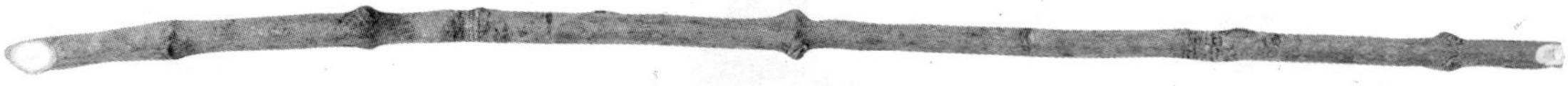

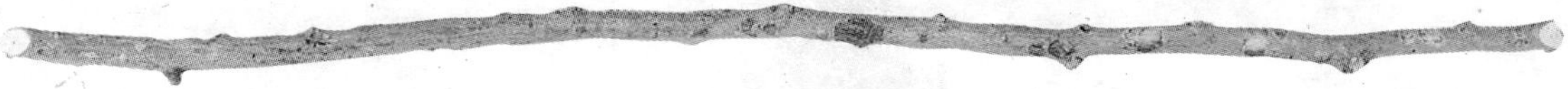

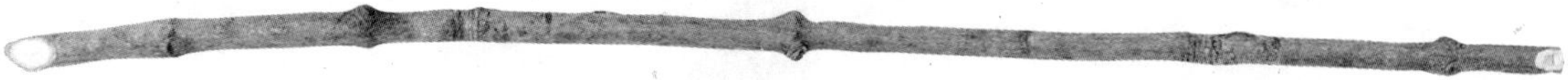

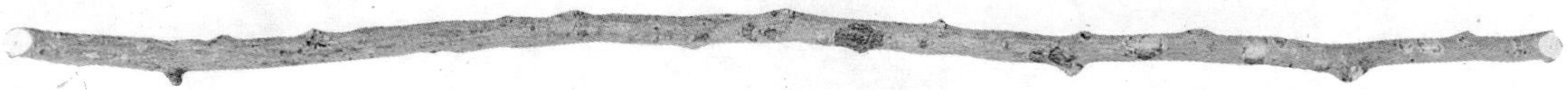

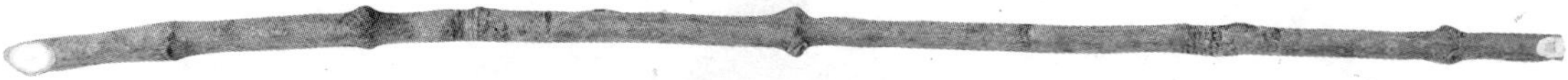

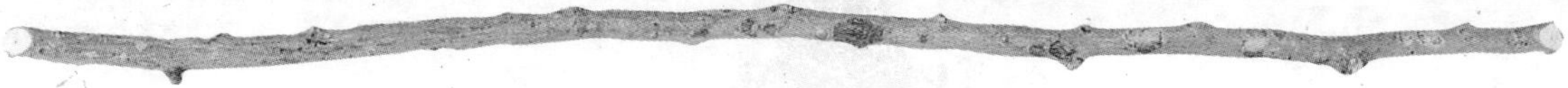

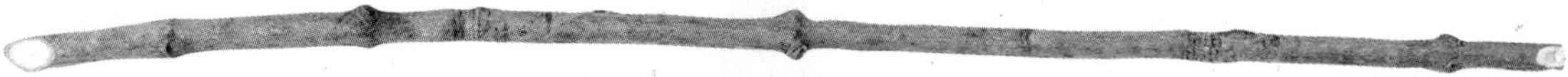

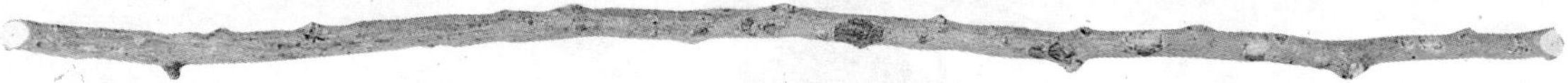

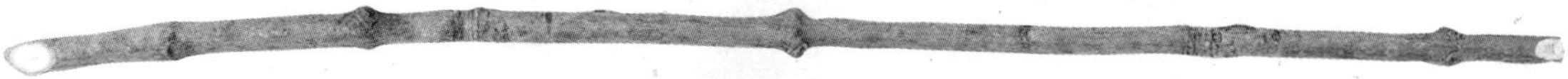

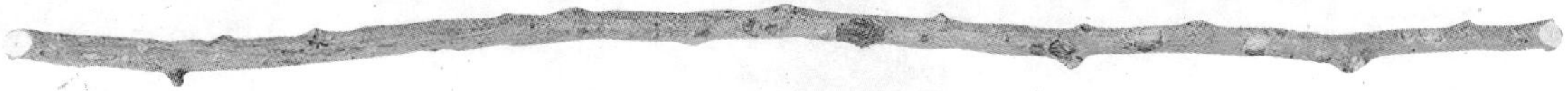

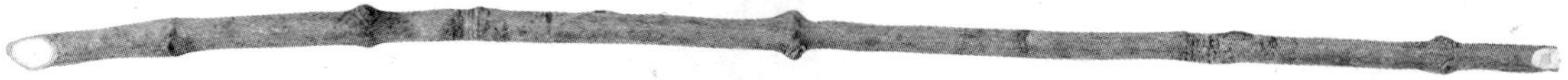

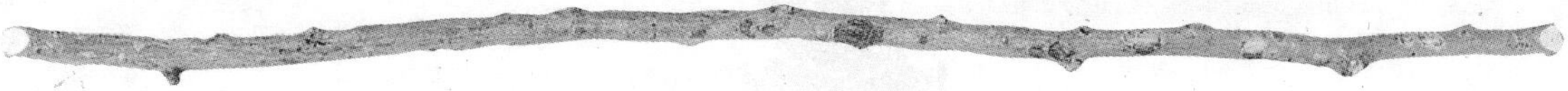

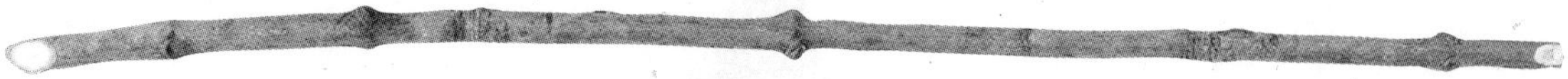

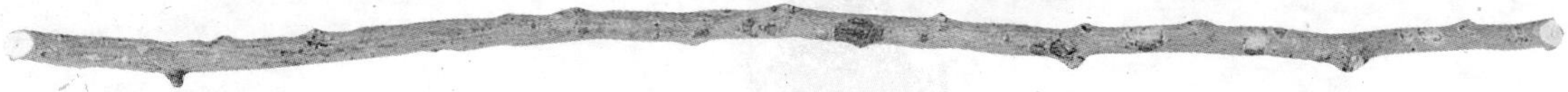

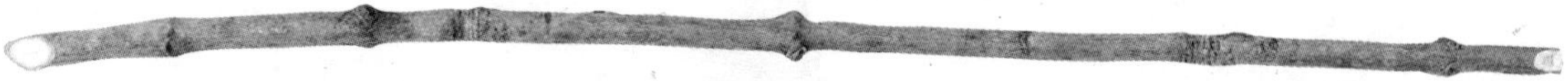

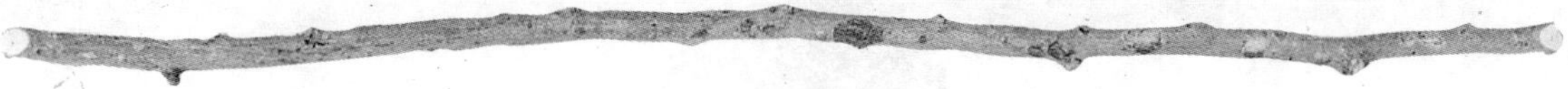

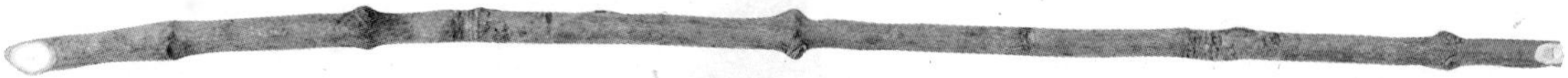

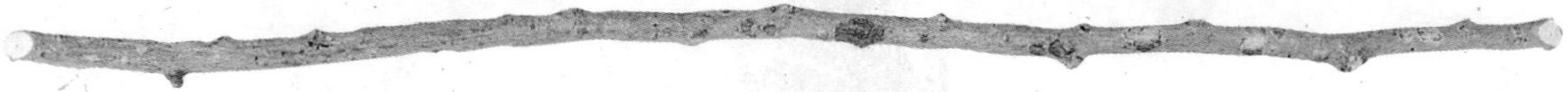

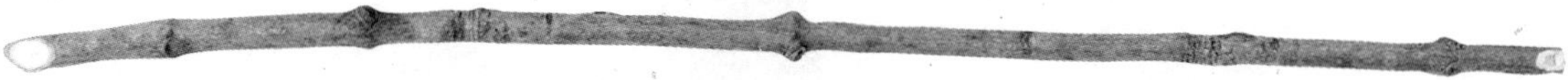

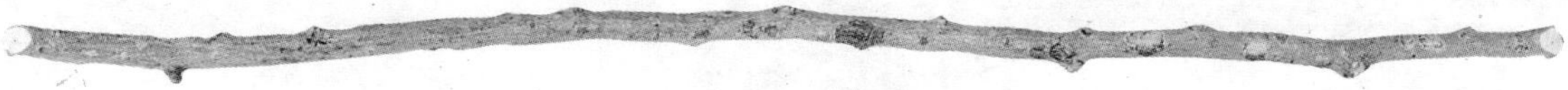

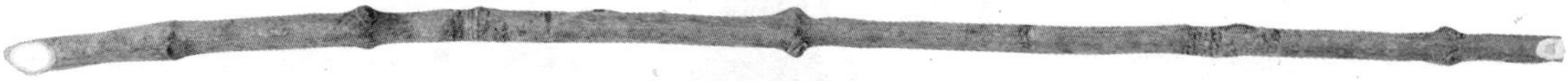

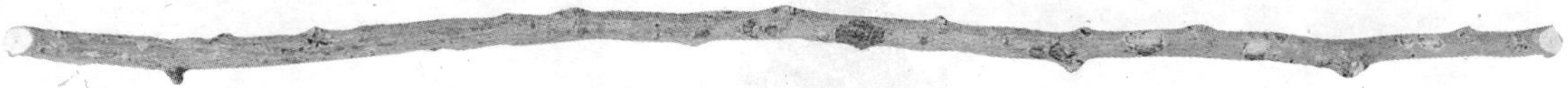

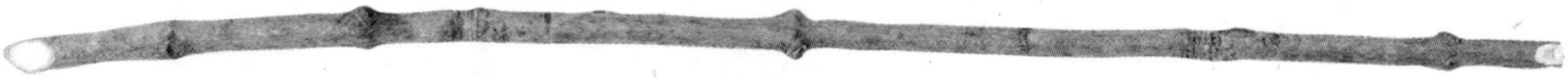

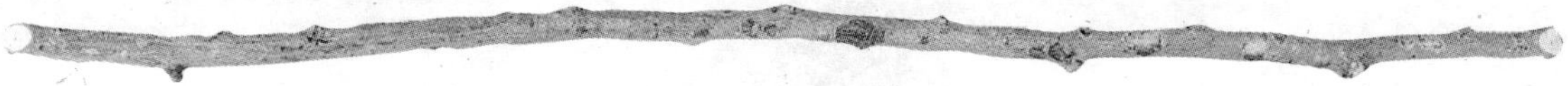

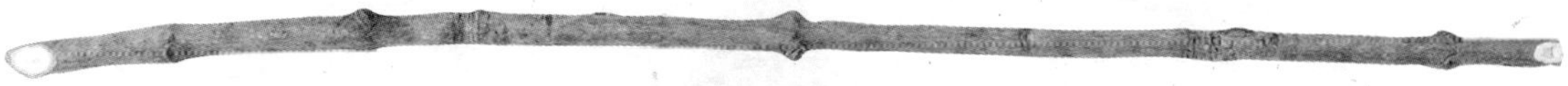

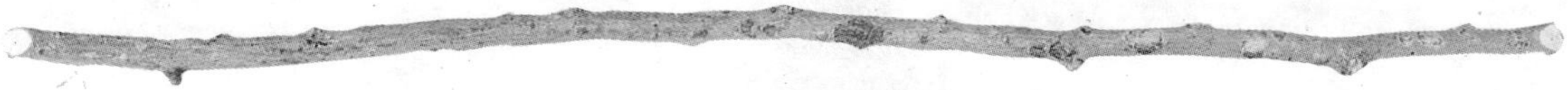

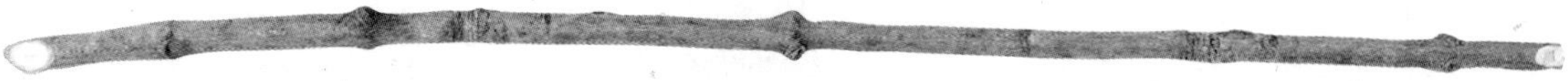

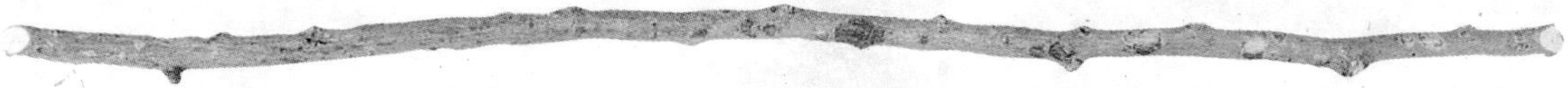

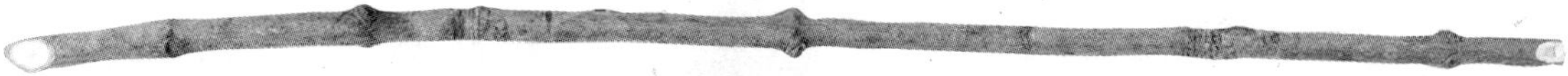

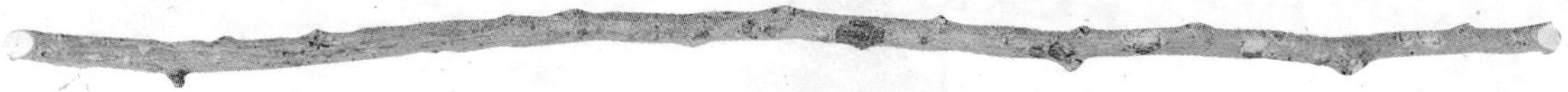

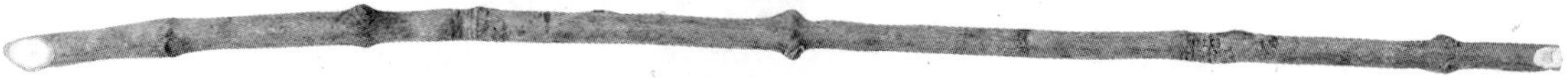

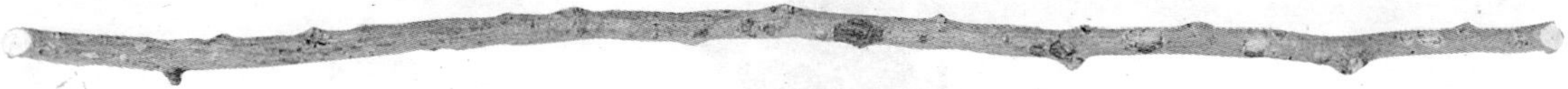

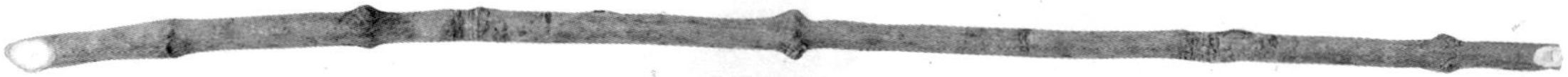

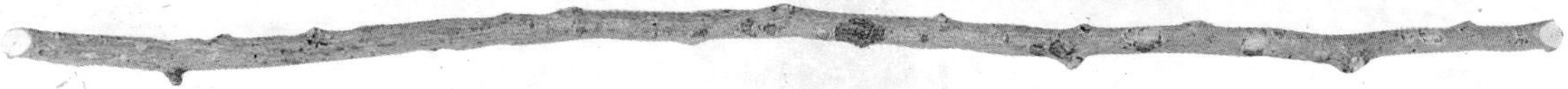

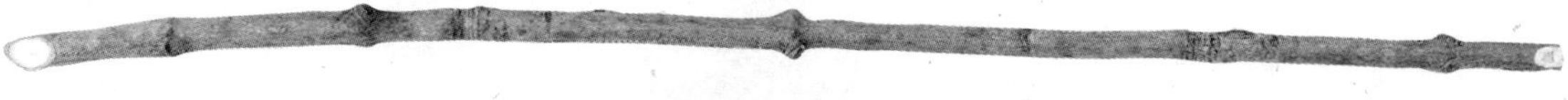

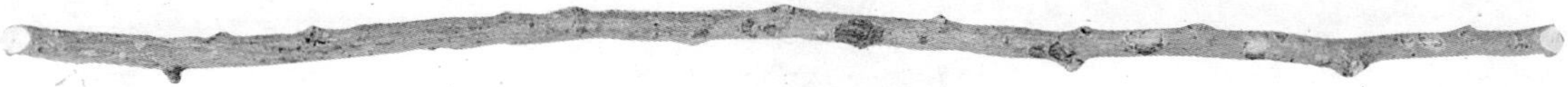

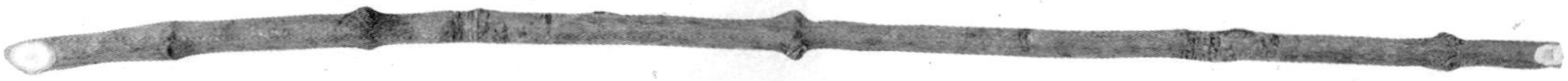

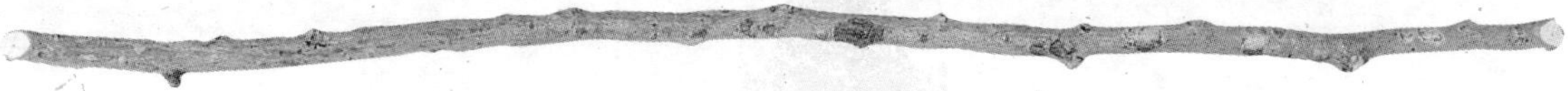

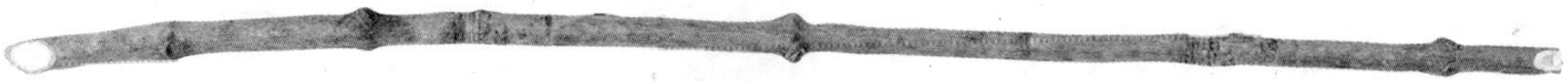

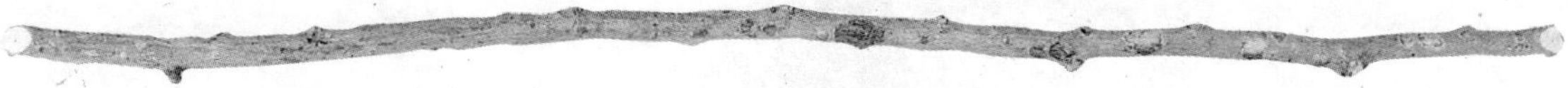

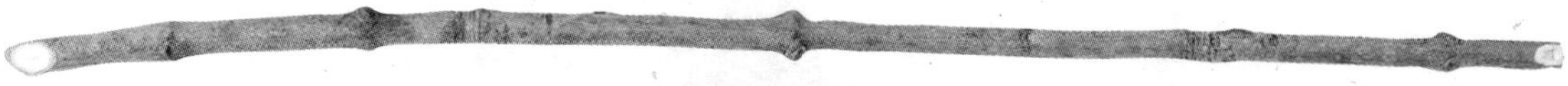

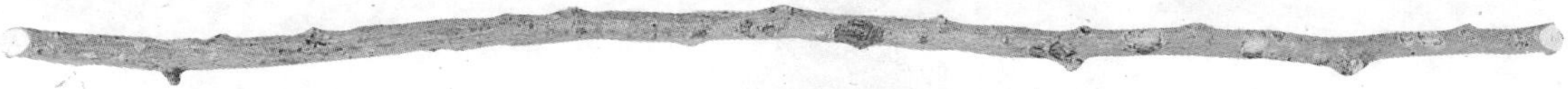

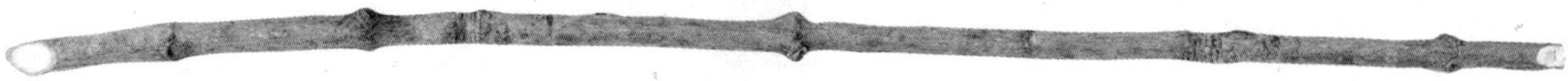

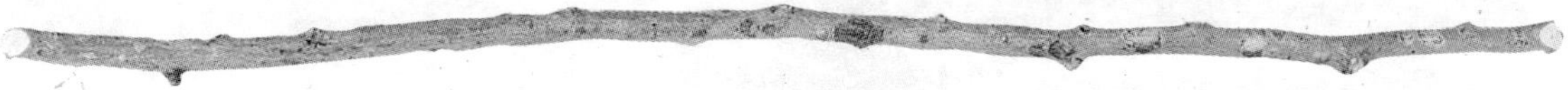

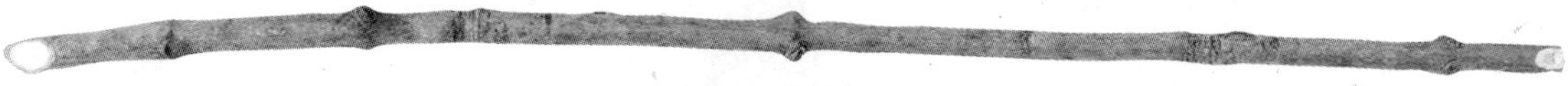

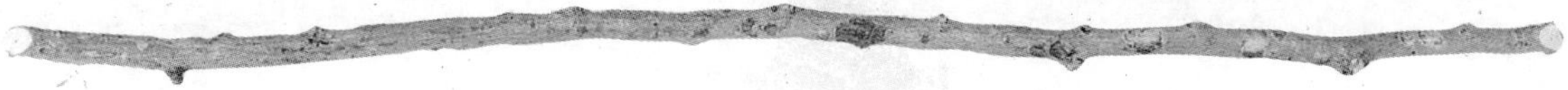

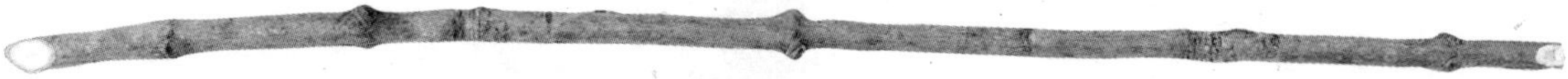

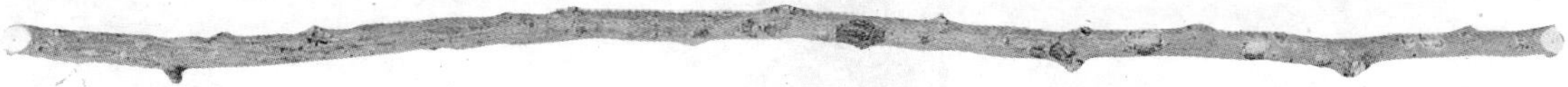

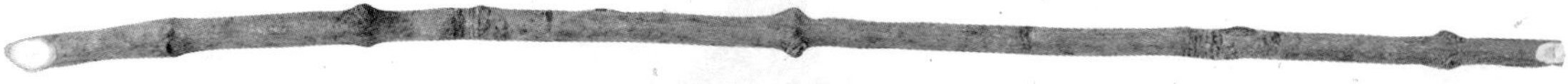

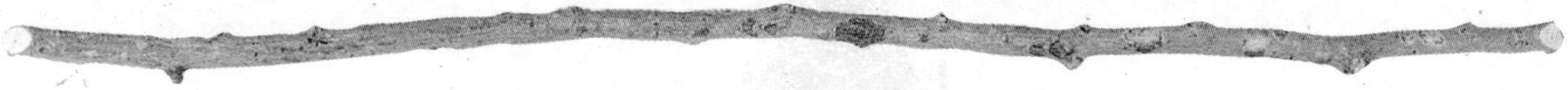

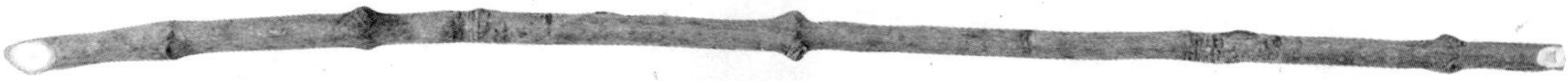

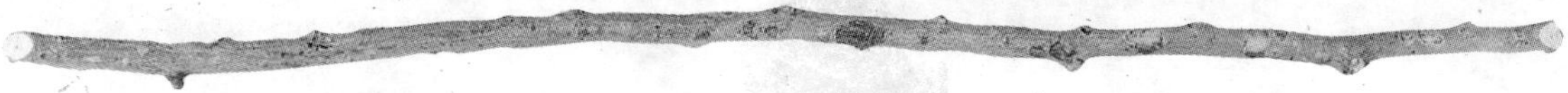

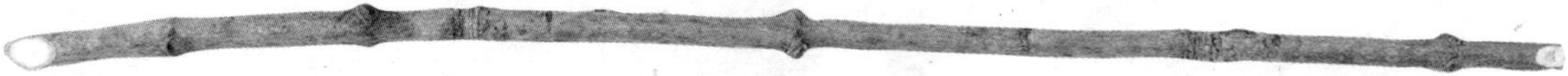

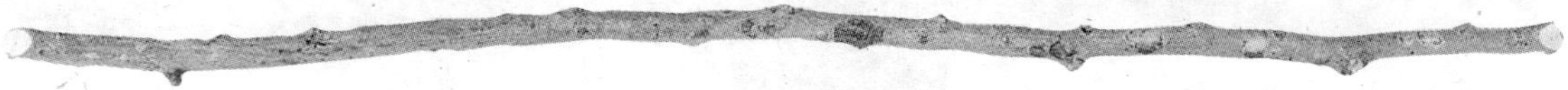

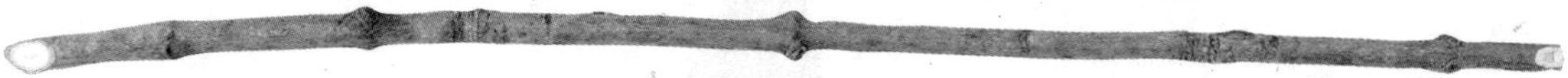

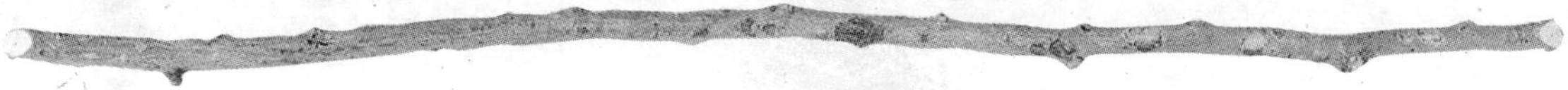

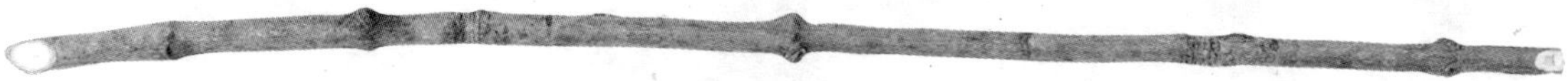

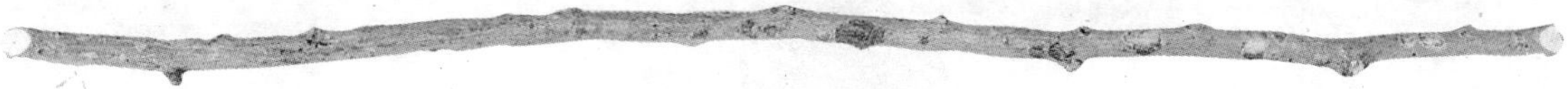

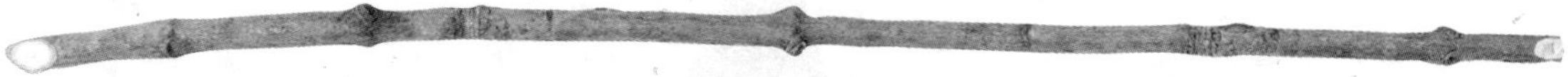

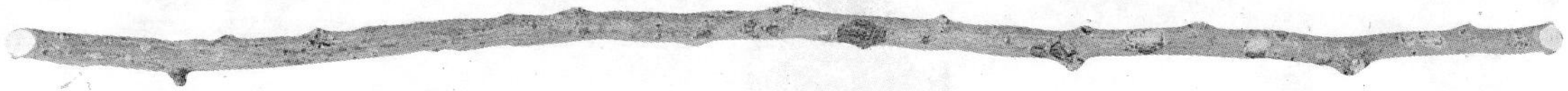

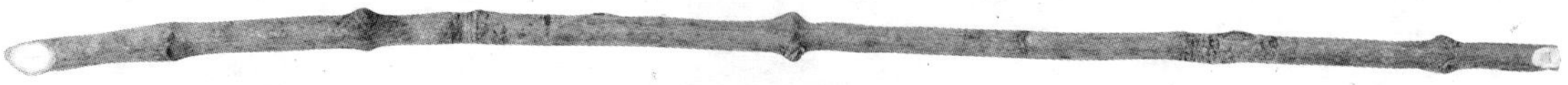

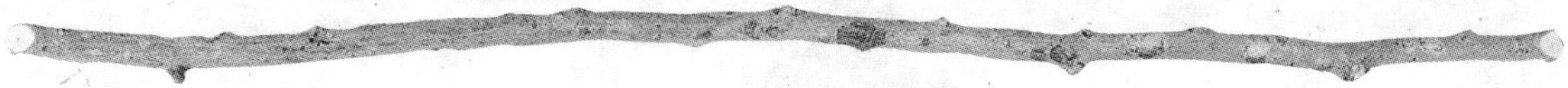

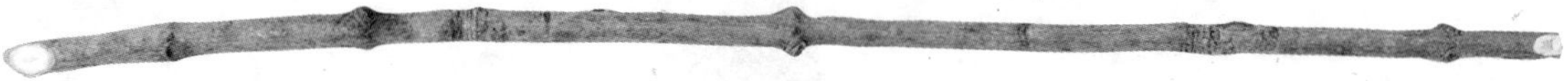

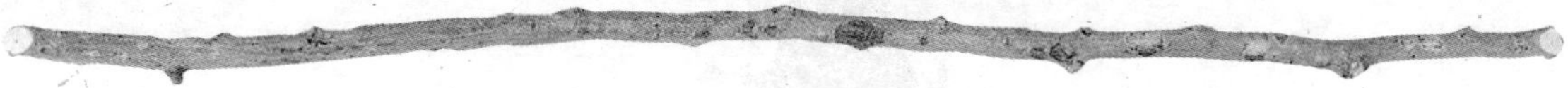

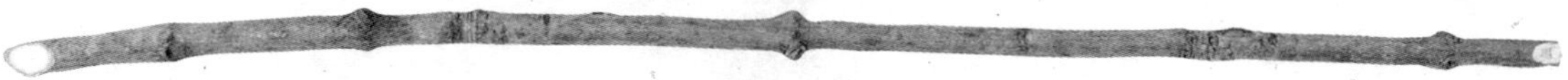

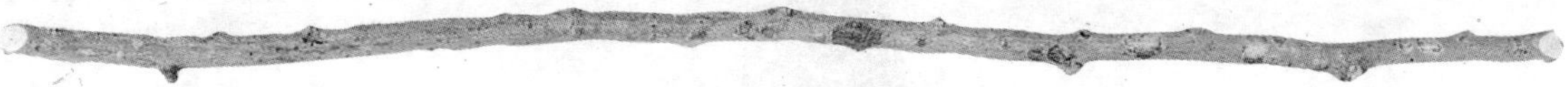

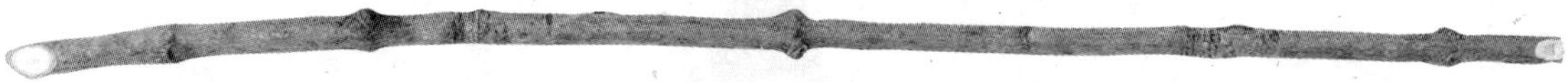